MW00416324

How to Carve a Duck Decoy

A Step-by-Step Guide for Beginners

by

BRIAN E. McGRAY

Drawings by Jean Hamilton

DOVER PUBLICATIONS, INC., *New York*

This book is dedicated to my wife Meredith,
whose love for what I do makes what I do possible!

WOODCARVING SUPPLIES

A full line of woodcarving supplies, including materials necessary to carve and paint a duck decoy, is available directly from the author. For a free catalog, write (sending self-addressed, stamped legal-size envelope) to:

Birds in Wood Studio
P.O. Box 2649
Meriden, CT 06450

Copyright © 1991 by Dover Publications, Inc.
All rights reserved under Pan American and International
Copyright Conventions.

Published in Canada by General Publishing Company, Ltd.,
30 Lesmill Road, Don Mills, Toronto, Ontario.
Published in the United Kingdom by Constable and Company, Ltd.,
3 The Lanchesters, 162–164 Fulham Palace Road, London W6 9ER.

How to Carve a Duck Decoy: A Step-by-Step Guide for Beginners
is a new work, first published by Dover Publications, Inc., in 1991.

Manufactured in the United States of America
Dover Publications, Inc.
31 East 2nd Street
Mineola, N.Y. 11501

Library of Congress Cataloging-in-Publication Data

McGray, Brian E.
How to carve a duck decoy : a step-by-step guide for beginners /
by Brian E. McGray ; drawings by Jean Hamilton.
p.   cm.
ISBN 0-486-26735-0
1. Wood-carving.   2. Decoys (Hunting)   I. Title.
TT199.75.M38   1991
745.593′6 — dc20   90-26815
                                      CIP

CONTENTS

Introduction

This book on carving a duck decoy is the result of the author's many years of carving, classroom teaching and experimenting with different techniques of carving. Over the years I have developed a simple method that can be learned by virtually anyone. Most books on the subject assume that the reader has expensive power tools, will use a mallet and chisels or has prior experience carving duck decoys. My method assumes only that the reader wants to carve a decoy, has a few very basic woodworking skills (like sawing and sanding) and tools and can find a small, sharp knife that he or she is comfortable using.

To learn the method, we will carve a male Mallard, the Mallard being the most widespread species of duck, familiar to everyone. Once learned, my method can be used to create woodcarvings of any other species of duck as well as other types of birds. The carvings can be used as working decoys or simply for decorative purposes and, with practice, can be made as realistic as the carver wishes.

Although carvers with some experience may pick up some helpful tips, this book was designed with the beginner in mind, guiding the would-be carver through the process of carving step by step. Each carving step is accompanied by a carefully thought-out illustration, and every term, every procedure, every technique is carefully explained. You'll learn how to choose, sharpen and hold your knife; how *not* to carve (the "Four Nevers of Woodcarving"); and how to set up the wood properly before you touch the blade to it. I have also included some information on different types of ducks, some advice on choosing wood and instructions for setting in eyes and painting your finished decoy. In addition, at the center of this book are patterns that you may cut out and use as templates for sawing out the body and head pieces of the Mallard that you will then carve to shape.

Basically, my technique works on the principle that if you carefully mark with penciled guidelines the wood you want to carve, then the process of carving becomes merely a matter of cutting to the guidelines. My method carefully controls the carving process by showing the carver, at each step, exactly where wood is to be removed and just how much. Just read all of the following instructions slowly and carefully, relax and have fun! It is my sincere hope that you will enjoy learning to carve a Mallard decoy as much as I have enjoyed preparing this book!

Before You Begin: A Few Words from Your Instructor

Before you begin, let me give you a few tips that will make the actual carving of your decoy a little easier. First, take a little time to read through this book. Especially if you are totally new to woodcarving, when you get to sections like "Sharpening Your Knife" and "Carving with Control," it is a good idea to practice these lessons before you begin the decoy.

Another important point is that each step of my method has been designed to follow the one before it and to lead into the next step. If for some reason you skip a step, or forget to apply something you learned earlier, you may find yourself not knowing what to do next. If this happens, simply backtrack until you find the step you missed, and then continue on.

Finally, once you have begun carving, first read the instructions for each step carefully and be sure you understand them and what specific goal you are aiming for before you put the step into practice.

The Four Nevers of Woodcarving

At any time you are working on your woodcarving project, there are four major things you should never do:

1. *Never* sit down to carve without having at least one hour of time to spend relatively free of interruptions.
2. *Never* sit down to carve without this book and any other reference material that you may be using.
3. *Never* sit down to carve without having a sharp pencil handy.
4. *Never* sit down to carve without making sure your knife is sharp.

The Patterns

The patterns that you use to cut out the basic shapes of head and body are very important. In fact they are the foundation of the whole project. If the patterns are drawn incorrectly there is little hope that the finished decoy will come out properly. When beginning, it is easiest simply to use the patterns I have provided with this book. Cut them out carefully. For longer life, they may be traced onto thin pieces of wood. When you have obtained a piece of wood for your decoy of the right type and size (more on wood below), place the patterns on the wood (the grain of the wood should run the long way) and saw around the shapes. This may be done with a handsaw but of course a power saw, such as a jigsaw or band saw, will be quicker. Before you cut out the profile of the head, drill a small hole (⅜″ in diameter for a Mallard) through the eyes, going completely through from one eye to the opposite one.

When you go on to carve decoys of other types of ducks, you may want to draw your own patterns. To help you design the patterns correctly, there are a few things you should know about ducks. Even if you are simply using the patterns I have provided, you will understand what you are doing more thoroughly if you know something about the birds represented by your carving.

Basically, most ducks fall clearly into one of two groups: puddle ducks (or dabbling ducks) and diving ducks. Puddle ducks are so called because they rarely feed in deep water, instead dipping their heads just under the surface of shallow water. On the other hand, diving ducks, like the scaups (or broadbills, as hunters call them), submerge themselves completely when feeding, sometimes diving all the way to the bottom of ponds to find food. They usually live in deeper water than puddle ducks.

Now what you should be aware of as a woodcarver is that the profile of a duck depends significantly on whether it is a puddle duck or a diving duck. Diving ducks, like the Bufflehead, swim in the water with their tails and breasts roughly in a straight line. Puddle ducks, like the Black Duck or any of the teals, all swim with their breasts low and their tails relatively high, giving them a slightly forward-tilted look compared to the divers. Figure 1 lists different species of puddle and diving ducks, and Fig. 2 shows the basic difference in their profiles.

Remember that good reference material always helps, whether you are drawing, carving or painting. Any of the currently available field guides to birds will depict many kinds of ducks.

Finally you should know that for each type of decoy you carve there are usually at least three patterns: two profiles (one for the head, one for the body) and a top view of the body. In this book I have added for the Mallard a separate profile for the tail and a top view of the head. Fig. 3 shows the profile patterns minimally given for a typical Mallard decoy. The profiles give the decoy its length, height and basic familiar ducklike shape. Fig. 4 shows the top view of a Mallard body. With the top view you trim excess wood from around the outside of the pattern as well as determining the width of the decoy.

Choosing the Wood

Many types of wood are available and many lend themselves to carving with a knife. They include sugar pine; white pine; red, yellow and white cedar; butternut — the list goes on and on. Choosing among these is a personal thing. What's hard to carve for one person may be easy for another, for any number of reasons. Some woods may also be suitable for certain types of carvings. The hardness of the wood is only one consideration.

One type of wood does deserve special mention:

SOME PUDDLE DUCKS	SOME DIVING DUCKS

Mallard
Black Duck
Wood Duck
Northern Pintail
American Wigeon
Teal (Blue-winged,
  Green-winged or
  Cinnamon)
Gadwall
Northern Shoveller
	Scaup (Greater or
	  Lesser) (also called
	  "Broadbill")
	Canvasback
	Redhead
	Goldeneye (Common
	  or Barrow's)
	Bufflehead
	Merganser (Common,
	  Red-breasted or
	  Hooded)
	Oldsquaw
	Ring-necked Duck
	Ruddy Duck

Fig. 1

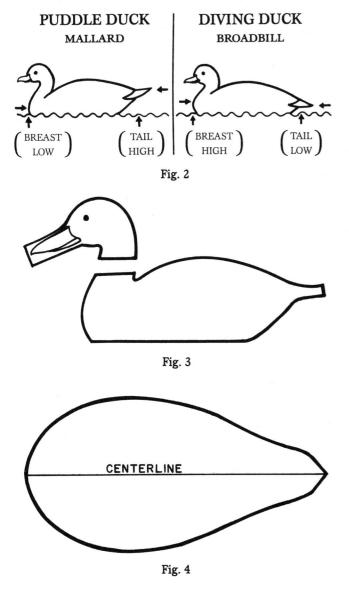

PUDDLE DUCK
MALLARD

DIVING DUCK
BROADBILL

(BREAST LOW)   (TAIL HIGH) (BREAST HIGH)   (TAIL LOW)

Fig. 2

Fig. 3

CENTERLINE

Fig. 4

basswood (or linden), a particular favorite of mine that I use for my own decoys and most of my other decorative carvings. Basswood is widely celebrated as an excellent wood for carving because it is soft and easy to cut, yet hard enough to hold fine detail. And when your basswood carving is finished it still looks like a carving in wood rather than ceramics or some other material.

But any number of woods will be fine for woodcarving providing they have been properly air dried or kiln dried. Be sure you check: don't use green — that is, wet or undried — wood. Look around your area to see what is available. Most of the woods I've mentioned can be found in a good lumberyard.

A final bit of advice: buy the wood in the thickness you need or a little larger. Avoid the mistake of trying to glue a hundred tiny pieces of wood together to make a two-inch-thick block. If you look around you will find pieces in at least that thickness.

Choosing a Woodcarving Knife

You don't have to carve very long before you become enchanted by woodcarving, finding the hours melt away as you slide a sharp edge of steel through a piece of wood. And it is at this edge of steel that our discussion of woodcarving knives begins.

There are probably as many opinions of what a good carving knife is as there are woodcarvers. But a few points should be helpful. Despite its beauty and resistance to corrosion, stainless steel is not the best metal for the blade of a carving knife. It doesn't keep an edge for very long, and it seems that you are always having to sharpen it. I like a knife that has a good carbon steel in it. Once sharpened, this type of steel keeps its edge much longer and will last a lot longer.

Other things to consider when looking at a carving knife are the blade's length and height, the sharpness of the point and the handle. For the beginner I offer this rule of thumb: if a knife is long and broad enough to carve wood at different angles, has a sharp point, keeps a sharp edge and fits in the hand well, then it is probably a good carving knife. If you can afford it, then it is probably the knife for you.

In the past, woodcarvers carved thousands of fine decoys using jackknives. If you have a jackknife (a large, strong pocketknife, as it would be more commonly called today) or any pocketknife that satisfies the above rule of thumb, it will probably do fine once you sharpen it. Remember my rule of thumb, and I'm sure that finding a good woodcarving knife won't be difficult.

Sharpening Your Knife

Probably just as important as selecting a good carving knife is knowing how to sharpen it. You will need a hard, wet sharpening stone, some oil of a type made for the purpose (ask in your local hardware store) and a razor strop (an old strip of leather will do).

Begin by placing a small quantity of oil on the stone. Then lay the knife blade against it (see Fig. 5). Slowly flatten the knife edge against the stone. Look closely and you should see a little ripple of oil appear as the cutting edge hits the stone flat. When that happens, press the knife firmly to the stone while slowly and carefully pushing the blade forward. It will look as if you're shaving a thin slice from the stone. *Carefully* repeat this step on the other side of the blade (pushing the blade only forward), and then repeat the entire process several times. The secret of success is first to think about what you're going to do, *then* do it very carefully.

Fig. 6 shows how to complete the sharpening process by stropping the knife. Lay one side of the blade flat onto the leather, press firmly, and slowly draw the knife backward. Turn the blade over and do this on the other side, always moving the knife backward only. Do this several times, and your knife should be sharp enough for carving. If it is not, repeat the above procedures until you are satisfied that your knife has a really sharp edge.

Carving with Control

Most people have at least once in their life taken a knife and whittled a piece of wood with it. Generally this is done by holding the wood in one hand while pushing the knife against it with the other. This type of rough carving doesn't permit much control and isn't really suitable for carving a decoy. Worse yet, it can be dangerous! True woodcarving with a knife, as

opposed to whittling, requires holding the knife in such a way as always to have maximum control over the edge or point of the knife.

The following instructions will show you some methods for holding and using a knife with maximum control. These procedures are safe when followed properly. Remember, however, that you must handle a sharp knife with prudence. Keep that in mind always!

The Anchor Hold (see Fig. 7). Place the knife handle in your hand where the fingers meet the palm.

Fig. 5

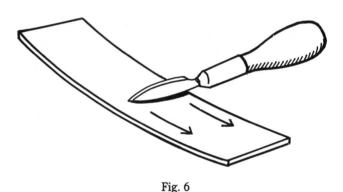

Fig. 6

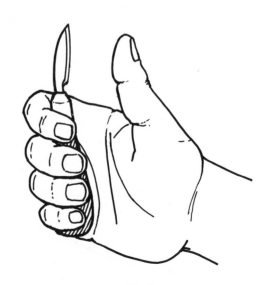

Fig. 7

Then close your fingers around the handle. The cutting edge of the blade should be facing the pad of your thumb. Before you begin to carve with this method, you must protect your thumb. This is done simply by wrapping a few adhesive bandages ("bandaids") around your thumb as shown in Fig. 8. As also seen in Fig. 8, to carve in this manner you must anchor the protected thumb on the wood. Then, with your fingers, you firmly pull the blade toward the thumb. Don't forget to end the cut before the blade hits your thumb.

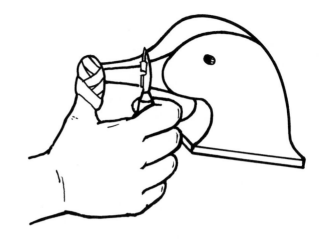

Fig. 8

Because the space between the knife blade and thumb is so short, and since the knife is being pulled by the fingers toward the thumb, the carver is always in control of the knife and should have no problem stopping it from hitting the thumb. If, despite all precautions, the blade does hit the thumb, the bandages should absorb the impact. Be sure to cover completely with the bandages all parts of the thumb that could conceivably be hit by the knife.

The Bridge Hold (see Fig. 9). The bridge hold also allows maximum control over the knife and is an excellent way to carve just about any part of a decoy, especially those hard-to-get-at places. As shown in Fig. 9, the knife handle should be placed in the hand diagonally, following the natural bend of the fingers. Then the thumb of that hand should be placed on the handle just next to where it joins the back of the blade. To complete the bridge, place the thumb of your other hand on top of the thumb that is resting on the handle. With this hold, the cutting edge of the blade should be facing *away* from you. Study the illustration and just practice holding the knife without carving, and you'll find you will soon get the knack of this hold.

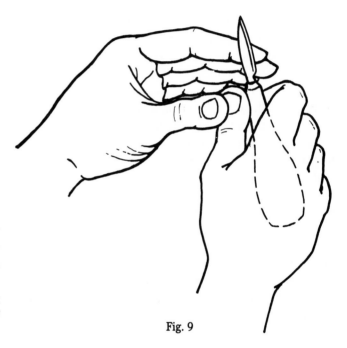

Fig. 9

Fig. 10 shows the bridge hold being used to smooth the eye trough of a decoy (we'll learn more about eye troughs a bit later) into the side of the head. The trick to carving with the bridge hold is to pivot the knife on the two thumbs. You can then cut in either of two ways. Either you can push the knife and the bottom thumb with the thumb that's on top, or you can use the top thumb as a brace, holding the bottom thumb in place and pivoting your wrist from side to side.

This method of carving works properly only if the connection between the thumbs is not broken. Learning to apply these holds properly is a matter of study, practice and time — the ingredients for doing anything well, in my opinion.

The Pencil Hold (see Fig. 11). I have saved the easiest way to hold a knife for last. The pencil hold is a simple yet very effective way to cut in the detail work on a decoy. As the name implies, you hold the knife

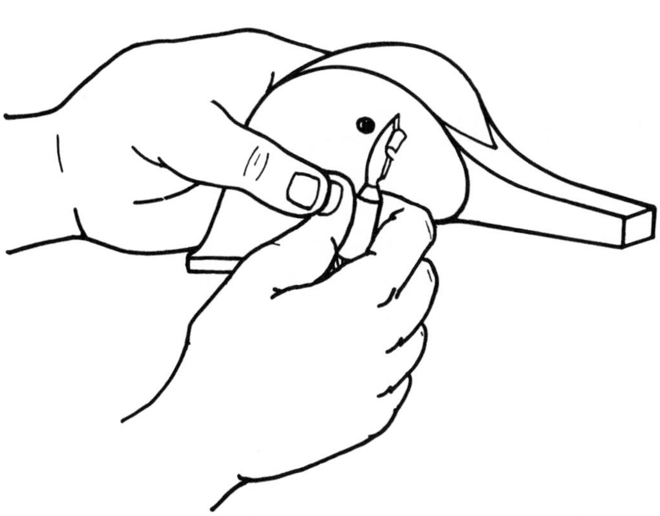

Fig. 10

exactly as you would a pencil. Rather than carving with the blade flat against an edge of the wood, with this hold you carve at a ninety-degree angle. (For those who don't remember what a ninety-degree angle is, the *point* of the blade should be aimed directly toward the flat surface of the wood so that the angle between the blade and the wood on one side of it is exactly the same as the angle on all other sides of the blade.) The pencil hold is used to cut directly into the wood in certain areas, such as where the bill meets the head (see Fig. 12).

The secret to maintaining control with the pencil hold is to have some part of the hand that holds the knife also touching the wood. Try using your little finger to make this connection, as shown in Fig. 12. It's really quite simple.

The key to carving with a knife using all the above methods is that the hand holding the knife is always somehow connected to the wood being carved. This reduces the length of the stroke of the blade, enabling the carver to exercise maximum control over the direction and depth of the cut at all times. The moment that this connection between knife-holding hand and wood is broken, the carver is whittling the decoy rather than truly carving it, a much less accurate — and less safe — way of cutting wood!

My teaching experience has shown the value of practicing on a spare piece of wood. This way many problems can be solved without ruining what might have become a fine piece of work. With a number of dry runs, when you don't have to concentrate on the form of the carving, many problems can be solved without cutting yourself or accidentally cutting away too much wood. With time you will master all of these methods and eventually may even develop a few of your own.

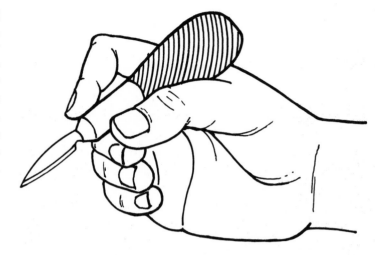

Fig. 11

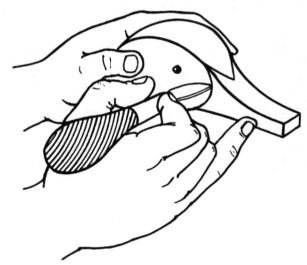

Fig. 12

Carving the Head

Before you actually cut into the wood with your knife, there are a few more things to prepare and procedures to keep in mind. We'll begin carving with the head. Start with the piece you have sawn out using the head patterns; its shape should resemble that shown in Fig. 13. Now with a ruler determine the exact center of the width of the top of the head. With an ordinary lead pencil make a few marks along this center and then connect the points with a penciled line. Extend this line to the back of the head and all the way to the tip of the bill, as shown in Fig. 13. Then

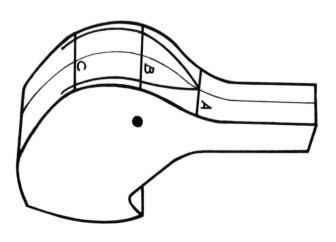

Fig. 13

6   *(Instructions continued after patterns.)*

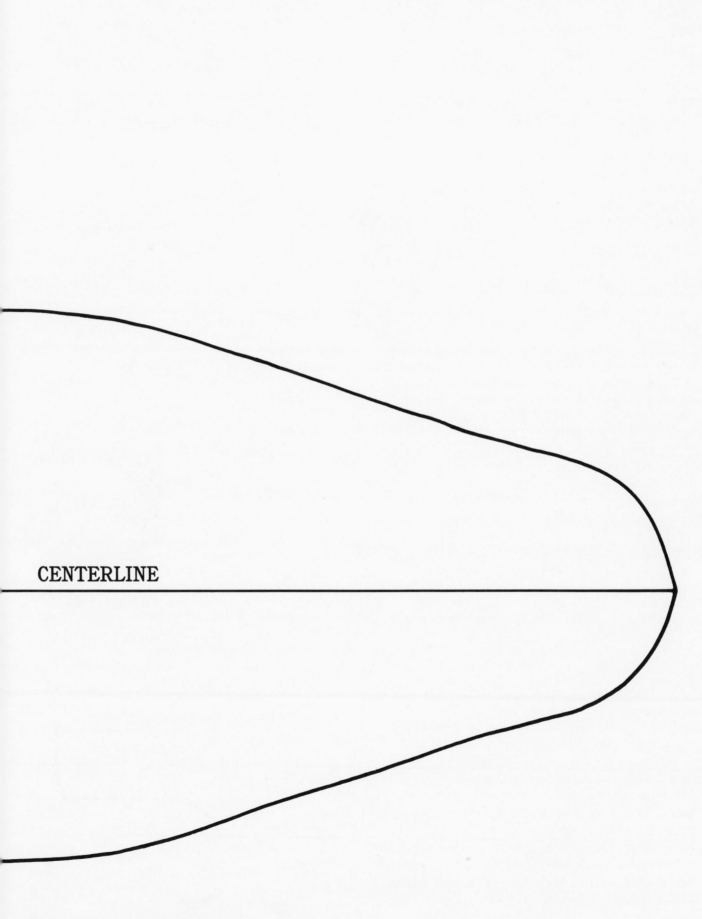

CENTERLINE

Remove staples to see and use patterns.

MALLARD DECOY PATTERNS

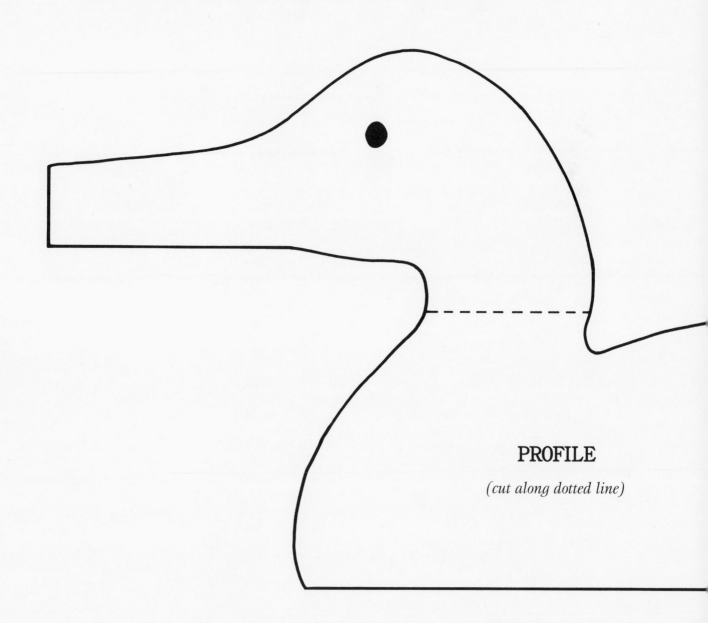

PROFILE

(cut along dotted line)

Remove staples to see and use patterns.

PATTERN SPECIFICATIONS

Species of Duck: Mallard (male)
Construction: 2-piece (head and body separate)
Dimensions:
Body: 12″ long × 2¾″ high × 5¾″ wide
Head: 5½″ long × 2⅝″ high × 1¾″ wide
Drill eye hole in head ⅜″ in diameter
    (drill after pattern is traced on
    wood but before shape is cut out)
Eye size and color: 10 mm brown

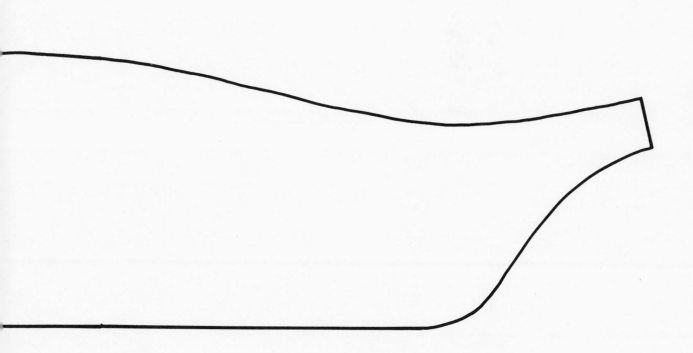

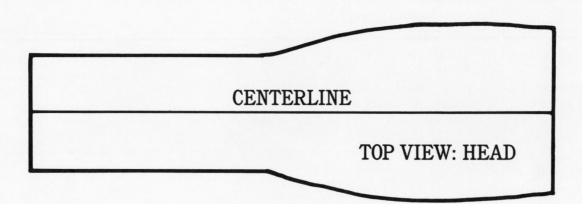

CENTERLINE

TOP VIEW: HEAD

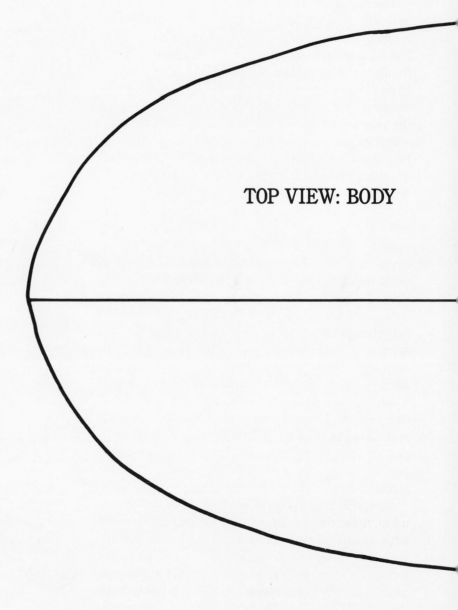

TOP VIEW: BODY

Remove staples to see and use patterns.

carefully extend it to all surfaces *under* the bill and in back of the head so that it goes all around the head, making a big circle. Draw this line very carefully and be sure it precisely divides the head in two. It will be your guide to symmetrical carving through the entire process. We will refer to it as the *centerline*.

Always remember throughout: first, think about what you are going to do; second, use the pencil as instructed; and finally, use the knife.

Now look again at Fig. 13. You will see three reference lines marked "A," "B" and "C," all drawn at right angles (a right angle is the same as a ninety-degree angle) to the centerline. Line A represents where the head meets the base of the bill; line B is aligned with the middle of the eye; line C is further back over where the cheeks will be. Now, referring to Fig. 13, draw lines A, B and C.

The width of the top of the decoy's head is shaped as it is because the head of a duck is narrowest where it meets the bill (corresponding to the placement of line A). It widens over the top of the head (line B) and, finally, is at its widest in the cheek area (line C). Notice the two lines in Fig. 13 that start where line A crosses the centerline and curve toward the back of the head to just past line C. These lines determine the width of the head for the reasons just mentioned. Now draw these lines. Make sure that they are exactly the same distance from the centerline and have the same curvature, or the head of your carving will be unbalanced. If they are not exactly right, erase them and try again.

Now study Fig. 14. This shows the proper way to carve the width of the head to the guidelines you just drew. Begin this cut at about a forty-five-degree angle (half of a ninety-degree angle) on the edge where the surfaces of the top and sides of the head meet (*always cut on edges unless specifically instructed otherwise*; more on this later). There are a few more things to keep in mind before you make the cut. Watch the grain of the wood. When it changes direction (which it usually does around the eye) the wood may tend to chip or split. To avoid this, you change direction too, and carve the other way. Whatever you do, do not cut past or into the guidelines. Always carve *up to* the penciled lines unless specifically instructed to do otherwise.

Now, referring to Fig. 14 and with these pointers in mind, make the cut. Take your time and think about what you are doing. Repeat the cut on the other side of the head. Again, be sure that both sides look the same.

You are now ready to prepare for carving the eye trough. This is a depression that extends down from the top of the head around the eye area, correspond-

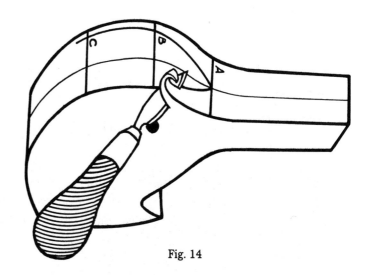

Fig. 14

ing to the actual shape of a duck's head. The eye trough covers the area extending from line A to just beyond line C, and from the top of the head to the bottom of the eye. The first step involves "coring" the eye. Put the point of your knife about ¼″ into the eye hole. If you position the knife as shown in Fig. 15, you can cut out the bottom half of the eye by holding the knife still and turning the head clockwise. Then cut out the top of the eye by turning the head counterclockwise.

By this procedure you will cut out a thin slice of wood all around the eye and create an *edge* between the eye and the side of the head. Look carefully at this edge. Before you created it, you could do little more than insert the point of your knife into the eye hole. Now you have created an *edge*—a noticeable angle between two surfaces, one surface running into the eye and the other running along the side of the head. By then cutting on this edge, you will create two new edges, each of which can also easily be cut. By cutting on edges, and creating new edges as you go, you will manage to scoop large quantities of wood from the surface of the decoy, in just the shape you want.

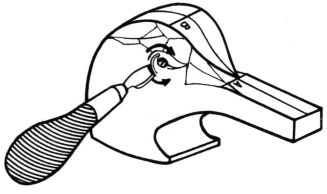

Fig. 15

These edges are what carving with a knife is all about. To understand further what I'm talking about, take a spare piece of wood, lay it down and try carving the flat surface of the wood. It's not easy to cut much out of it! *Learning to carve edges and create new edges as you go is the secret to all woodcarving with a knife.* As you carve, don't let yourself be distracted by all the chips you are making. Instead, train yourself to concentrate on the shape you are trying to create. With practice and patience you will gain confidence, learn to create edges where you need them and learn how to use these edges to your best advantage.

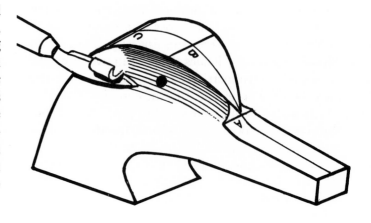

Fig. 16

Now you are ready to carve out the eye trough. Start by cutting outward along any side of the circle of edges you made when you cored the eye. Keeping in mind the shape you are striving for, continue to scoop out wood by the method of creating and cutting edges. Slowly work outward from the eye on both sides and up to the top of the head. Fig. 16 should give you an idea of how to proceed. When you are finished, the eye hole should be slightly recessed. As you go, test for this by the following method. Hold the head so that you are looking at the centerline on the top of the head, with the bill facing forward. If the eye hole is just barely visible, and the cut-out area runs from line A to just beyond line C, then you've probably been cutting out the eye trough correctly. Cut out eye troughs on both sides. Remember as you go to concentrate on the shape, not the chips. And why rush? Woodcarving is supposed to be fun!

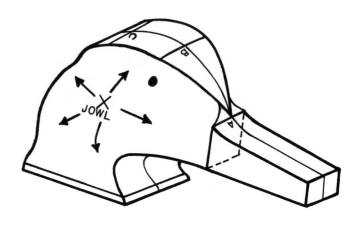

Fig. 17

After you have cut the eye troughs to your satisfaction, check the centerline. Darken it if necessary, for we will soon need to refer to it again. Now we set up for the starburst cut. To do this, first extend line A all around the bill (see Fig. 17). Next, draw a line all around the base of the neck. On most decoys, this line should be about ¼″ above the base. Finally, using Fig. 17 and any other reference materials as a guide, determine where the jowl — that is, the cheek — of your decoy should be. After the head has been finished, the jowl will be the highest point on each side. Mark the jowl with an "X."

The starburst cut is begun on one of the edges at the front of the neck. As shown in Fig. 18, you will cut up and around the underside of the face toward the base of the bill. As you cut, keep in mind the rounded shape of the neck, and do not cut past the centerline or the guideline around the bill. Then work your edges toward the eye trough, the back of the head and down around the neck. All the while, work around the jowl that you marked with the "X." All these areas should run smoothly into each other, creating a gently rounded cheek.

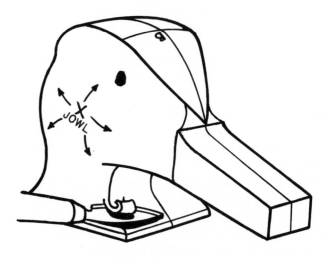

Fig. 18

8

As you are working, keep in mind that in most woods the direction of the grain will begin to change as you get somewhere behind the eye. You'll know when this is happening because the wood will begin to split when you try to carve it. When this happens, just turn the knife around and carve in the opposite direction. As with any procedure, learning to carve with the grain takes a little time and practice. Don't expect to get everything perfect the first time. Each decoy you carve will be better than the one before it. If you truly master one step or type of cut with each project, that will be reasonable progress.

Remember, as you do the starburst cut, the jowl should run smoothly into the eye trough, the back of the head and the neck. Also, as you go, check to see that the jowl has remained the highest point on the side of the head (simply look down at the top of the head as you did to check the eye trough). When you have completely finished one jowl, begin the other, and, using the centerline as a guide, check repeatedly to keep the two sides of the head looking the same. Once you have clearly in mind everything you are aiming for, you can actually begin the cutting.

Next we will begin preparing for the carving of the bill. A few words of caution before you begin. The bill is a relatively small portion of your decoy and its shape includes many sharp curves. Cutting the angles on the bill can be difficult. When cutting at an awkward angle, if you are not careful your knife may slip and you may cut yourself. I have designed this book to help you through difficult cuts such as those involved in carving the bill. I will warn you when the tricky cuts are coming. If you meet me halfway by reading my instructions carefully and paying attention to what you are doing, you should have no problem.

Let's begin the bill. First be sure that your centerline is clearly marked all around the bill. Now, on the *bottom* of the bill (see Fig. 19), draw two lines on either side of the centerline and parallel to it. These lines should begin at the base of the bill (marked by the continuation of line A under the bill, not shown in Fig. 19) and should begin to curve, to meet where the centerline meets the tip of the bill, forming a semicircle at the front of the bill. The exact width of the bill — that is, the distance between the parallel lines — is determined by the top-view pattern for the head. Check to be sure that the guidelines for the width of the bill are the same distance from the centerline.

Now refer to Fig. 20 to get an idea of how to carve the basic shape of the bill. Hold the knife so the blade is parallel to the side of the bill. You may find it easier to begin at the corners and round out the front of the bill first. You can begin the back of the cut at the base

of the bill, cutting in along the extension of line A and forward along the lines marking the bill width. Carefully smooth together all cuts. Remember to cut *up to* the penciled lines, don't cut them away. When you are finished, the width and the curve at the tip of the bill should be cut out. When you make further cuts later on, be careful not to cut through the reference lines under the bill, or you may end up with a crooked or overly narrow bill, spoiling the head and all the fine work you've done up to this point. *Think* before you cut!

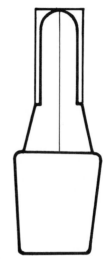

Fig. 19

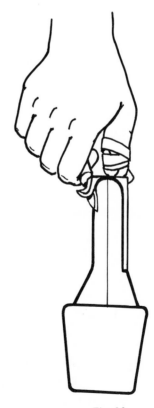

Fig. 20

9

The next setup is for carving the top of the bill. Refer to Fig. 21. Starting from in front of each eye, draw two lines to form a "V." The lines should meet on the centerline about three-quarters of the way down the top of the bill. Again, these lines should be straight and look the same on each side. Check by holding the head so the bill is facing you. Fig. 22 shows how to cut the top of the bill. Begin at line A and cut up to the "V" you just drew. Cut up to the centerline and the bottom reference lines. When viewed from the front looking toward the head, the bill should end up looking tent-shaped. Whatever you do, do not cut past the bottom guidelines, the "V" or the centerline. Cutting past the bottom guidelines is a mistake commonly made by beginners, which is why I am repeating this warning.

The next cut is made on top of the "V." This cut is a little tricky. You are cutting with the knife laid practically flat against the wood (you have seen how hard this is), and for the first time you will be cutting away a part of the centerline. Study Fig. 23. This cut starts behind the base of the bill and ends at the top of the "V." It should be made in a single shaving stroke, flaring up at the end, rather than with a series of small cutting strokes.

Start by laying the cutting edge across the top of the head a little behind line A. Now with one smooth, slow power stroke, cut a flat area up to the point of the "V." End the cut by carefully turning the blade up, away from the bill. This cut establishes the slant on the top of the bill. Check to see that it is level and the same on both sides by pointing the bill toward you.

Before you proceed, redraw all the lines you have cut away (see Fig. 24). Now you have to add two more lines on each side of the head: a curved line at the place where the bill joins the head, and a little straight line joining the curved line to the bottom of the bill. Study Fig. 24 to see just how these lines should look.

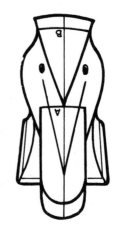

Fig. 21

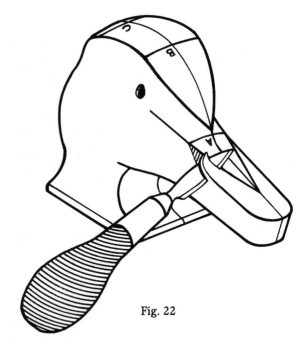

Fig. 22

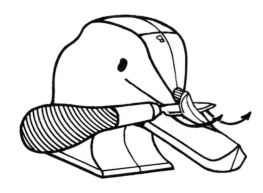

Fig. 23

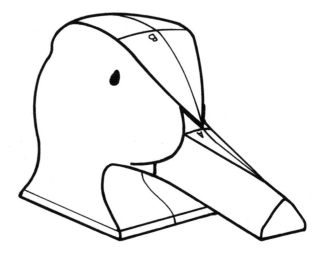

Fig. 24

Additional reference material really helps here. To be sure these lines are the same on both sides, hold the head with the bill facing away from you and place the nail of the index finger of each hand on the opposite sides along the farthest part of the curved line. Your fingers should be opposite each other. Do the same at the points where the curved lines meet the little straight lines. When you are satisfied that your lines are even, it's time to move to the next setup step.

Study Fig. 25. On the bottom side of the bill draw two "V"s. One should connect line A (not shown in Fig. 25), which you drew at the base of the bill, to the centerline. The other "V" is at the tip of the bill and should connect two corners of this tip with the centerline. Fig. 25 makes it perfectly clear how these "V"s should look. Notice that they point toward each other. Now, between the "V"s, about halfway down the length of the bill, draw a straight line across the bill.

At this point, it's a good idea to check *all* your guidelines. Once you carve the areas you've marked, it's too late to adjust the lines.

In the next few steps your carving will again involve placing your knife at a ninety-degree angle to the wood. If you don't remember what a ninety-degree angle is, go back and check my explanation. It is very important to keep the knife blade exactly at this angle without tilting it to either side. By moving it off just a little bit, you will change the angle at which the line gets cut in and ruin the carving. Again, some

practice cutting at a ninety-degree angle on a spare piece of wood will make carving a lot easier later on.

Some further words of caution before we go on. When you cut straight into the bill at a ninety-degree angle, use the pencil hold (which you may want to review now). Also, to avoid the danger of cutting yourself, when you trace the penciled lines with the knife, don't press too hard. If necessary, instead go over the same line several times using lighter pressure. And when you make a cut that goes to the end of the wood, as in the "V"s that you just drew in on the bottom of the bill, reduce the pressure on the knife point as your cut is ending. Always remember, also, that the two free fingers of the hand holding the knife should be kept firmly anchored at all times to the piece of wood being carved. It doesn't hurt, either, to keep reminding yourself to check the sharpness of your knife blade — especially, for these steps, the blade point. All of these steps will be unnecessarily difficult if you are using a dull knife! If you follow these instructions carefully, practice before you carve and exercise reasonable caution and a little common sense, your wood carving will be simple, safe and fun!

Now let's begin carving the bottom of the bill (see Fig. 26). *Remember to be very careful when cutting at an angle.* Start at the "V" closest to the neck. With the point of your knife (holding the knife at exactly a ninety-degree angle) trace over the penciled lines on the "V." Cut down about 3/16″. Then move your knife

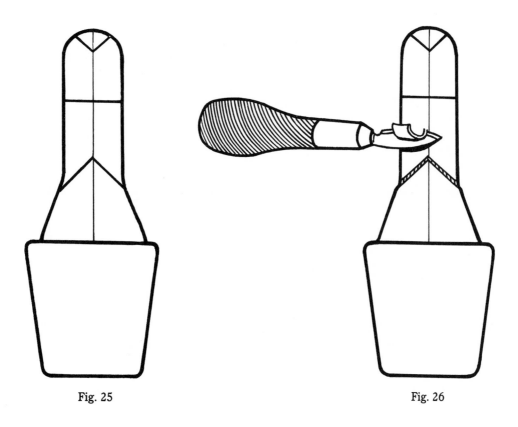

Fig. 25   Fig. 26

down so the whole blade is over the line you've just cut. Go forward a little bit, tilt the knife and cut out a little wedge of wood. This will give you an edge for further carving. Do this on both sides, as shown in Fig. 26. Now carve by working your edges forward up to the line you drew across the middle of the bill. The aim of this step is to cut away a little wood and make this segment of the wood perfectly flat. Naturally, you will have to cut away the centerline in doing so. Check this by looking straight down the bottom of the bill (to see that both sides are the same) and by looking at the bill from the side. The part you carved should be flat from the "V" near the neck to the line across the bill.

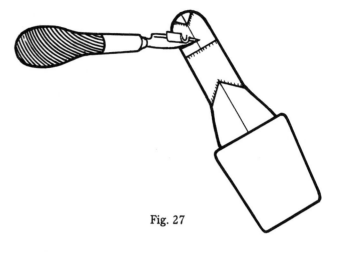

Fig. 27

Now let's finish the bottom of the bill. *Again, cut with caution!* (See Fig. 27.) Cut into the lines of the smaller "V" with the point of your knife held at a ninety-degree angle, just as you did before, only not quite so deep (or you will carve the front of the bill too high). Again, cut out a little wedge and carve the edges back to the line across the bill. This time, don't carve flat but cut so the front portion of the bill looks as if it's tilting up when the head is held upright. Go slow and easy! Finish up the bottom by placing the knife blade across the little "V" about halfway to the bill tip, and, with the blade tilted at a forty-five-degree angle, gently slice off the point of the "V." Don't overdo it! Smooth over all border areas so the bottom of the bill starts to slope gently up (seen from an upright position) toward the tip. Once again, *be careful* when you make those angle cuts!

Next, turn the head over to work on the top of the bill. Refer to Fig. 28. Begin by tracing with your knife point along the curved lines and the little straight lines you drew earlier, as well as the little "V" created by the guidelines you drew much earlier, where it joins the curved lines. The illustration should make this clear. Once again cut at a ninety-degree angle, always *cutting with caution*. The depth of this cut depends on the particular decoy you are carving. As a rule of thumb, cut just deep enough so that, when you have cut away wood from the bill, the bill will look as if it is a separate piece of wood stuck into the head. Once again, cut out little wedges of wood to begin, then work your edges down the bill, staying within the guidelines as shown in Fig. 28. At this point, the bill should still be flat (actually with a slight depression) on top in the space between the two "V"s.

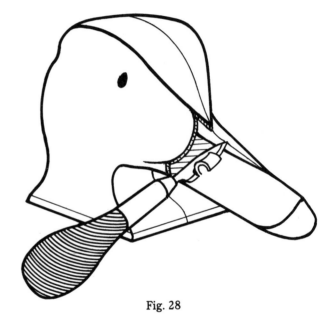

Fig. 28

You are now ready to finish the top of the bill. This is done in two stages. (Refer to Fig. 29.) First, round out the tip of the bill. Simply cut edges in the usual way until there are no more edges to carve. Next, starting at the point of the long "V" that you drew

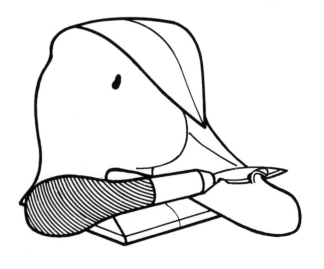

Fig. 29

much earlier, smooth out the flat area so it gently curves toward the centerline. Also smooth this area into the front portion of the bill that you just rounded out. Examine the bill all around to check for evenness and smoothness. It should be shaped like the bill in Fig. 30.

If you examine Fig. 30, you'll notice that an additional line is shown drawn in. This line connects the point where the curved line joins the little straight line, on one end, to the point where the bill sweeps upward about halfway along its length, on the other end. Carefully draw in this line. It marks the separation between the upper and lower mandibles of the bill. Draw one to match on the other side. Check that they are the same by the method of pointing the bill away from you and holding the head by the fingernails on the farthest part of these two opposite lines.

When you are satisfied, you are ready to cut out the lower mandible of the bill. *Be careful, as you will begin with angle cuts.* (See Fig. 31.) Trace along the lines you have just drawn, as well as the little straight lines, with the point of your knife held at a ninety-degree angle. Now cut out a little wedge next to the little straight line to create an edge. Carve down the area shown in Fig. 31. The lower mandible should show as an area slightly recessed under the upper mandible. As you carve these areas (remember to carve both sides), be sure to avoid sticking the point of your knife into the upper mandible.

We are now in the home stretch! The next cuts do not need to be set up, since they involve rounding out various parts of the head. Start with the edges of the crown as shown in Fig. 32. As you round out the crown and smooth over the edges, remember that in most woods the grain has a tendency to change direction behind the eye. Also remember that the centerline should remain visible until the end, marking the highest point of the head.

Next, gently smooth over all the borderlines between the head and the bill. Don't overdo this, as the bill should still look as if it is a separate piece of wood stuck into the head. Finally, on the underside of the bill, take a different approach: there, the border of the head and bill should be accentuated a little by slightly undercutting the "V" as in Fig. 32. Do this very carefully. Don't be impatient. You may ruin all your previous work or cut yourself. Look over the entire head and bill to make sure that both sides are the same and all areas that should be rounded out look smooth.

Congratulations! You have just completed the head, the most difficult part of a decoy to carve. What's more, the method you have learned can be used to carve the head of any type of duck decoy!

Fig. 30

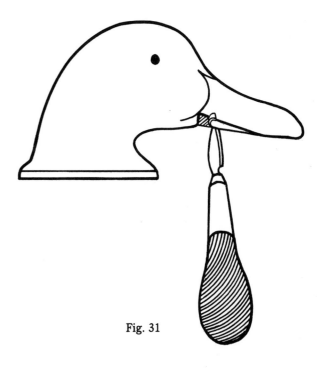

Fig. 31

Fig. 32

Carving the Body

The body of a duck decoy is not as difficult to carve as the head, simply because you don't have to make as many angle cuts. Before you start, make sure that the shape is sawn out properly according to the profile and top-view patterns. As you did for the head, draw a centerline on top of the body and extend it completely around the piece. Be sure that this line is in the *exact* center, or the body will end up lopsided.

Turn the piece so the bottom is facing up. Now, using your pencil and ruler, make little marks ½″ from the outside edges of the bottom, except on the tail part (see Fig. 33). Keep these marks a couple of inches apart. (Naturally, decoys smaller than the Mallard we are working on will need marks a little closer to the edge, say ¼″; use common sense.)

Next, connect the marks you've made with a curved line, following the basic shape of the body. When you approach the end that will be the breast of the duck (opposite the tail), curve the lines smoothly to meet where the centerline meets the front edge. Study Fig. 33 to get the idea. Be sure to draw both sides exactly the same way. It is important that the lines on both sides are smoothly curved and look exactly alike, because these are reference lines that will contribute a great deal to the final appearance of the decoy.

When you are satisfied that your reference lines are correct, place your knife at a forty-five-degree angle and carve along the outer edges of the body from the breast to the border of the tail. Carve by creating and cutting edges, as you just learned when carving the head. As you go, carve up to but not into your reference lines. Fig. 34 shows how this should be done. Cut so the area you've carved is smoothly rounded, but leave edges along the outer borders of the area you've carved. Carve both sides to look the same.

Here are a couple of pointers to follow while carving. As you approach the midpoint of the wood, the grain direction may begin to change. If this happens, the wood will begin to split. To counteract this, change the direction of your carving at that point. Also, be careful when carving the ends of the body. The end grain is usually very hard, and it is easy for the knife to slip.

Once you've carved the bottom of the body, turn the body over. We will now set up the next carving steps. First, draw a line at right angles to the centerline, all the way around the border of the tail and the main part of the body (see Fig. 35). Next, take the head that you just finished carving and place the base of the

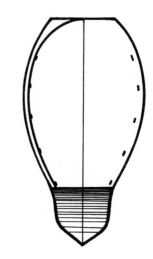

Fig. 33

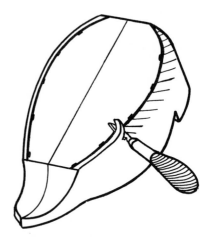

Fig. 34

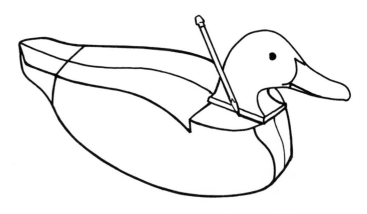

Fig. 35

14

neck where it will be on the finished decoy. Position it exactly on the neck seat of the body as shown in Fig. 35. Take your time to do this accurately, using the centerline as a guide. Once the head position is marked and carving proceeds, the carving will be ruined if the head has not been placed properly. When you have positioned the head to your satisfaction, draw a line right on the neck seat all around the base of the neck. Be careful not to move the head as you draw this line. Check again and make sure that this outline correctly shows the head position you want. If everything looks right, you can go on to carve the sides and top of the body.

Refer to Fig. 35 again. Notice the top edges of the sides of the body. Begin carving on these edges and work toward the centerline. The smoothly curved sides should begin to look like those in Fig. 36. Carve up to but not into the neck seat. Also work down both sides of the body. Before you get midway down the sides, turn the body over and work the bottom edges toward the middle of the sides so your carved-out top and bottom portions of the sides smoothly meet.

As you carve the sides, keep the following things in mind. The final shape you are working toward should look basically like the rounded body of a submarine. Streamlined for more efficient motion through the water, submarines and ducks are similarly shaped! Your decoy should have this shape too! Remember also, never carve flat (except at certain times when you are specifically instructed to do so). Always carve edges, creating new edges and working them in the direction you want. And watch your guidelines, including the centerline. Carve up to but never into or past these lines (again, with the exception of a few instances when you are specifically instructed to cut away guidelines). Keep the carving on both sides of the centerline the same, handle your knife with care, adjust to any change of grain direction, study the illustrations, take your time and use a little common sense, and you should have no problem carving the body.

The major carving step left is cutting in the tail. First draw some guidelines on the side of the tail (see Fig. 37). Measuring the halfway point on the border of the side and end of the tail, draw a centerline on the side from there to the base of the tail. Do this on each side. Then draw one line on each side of each centerline, parallel to it and about ⅛″ away (measurements will be a little different on other types of decoys). Extend these lines also from the tip of the tail to where the tail meets the body. Be sure that these lines are always the same distance from the side cen-

terlines. Do this on each side of the tail, and check to be sure that the lines look the same on each side. Do this by holding the body with the tail facing you.

Now look at Fig. 38. Begin carving the tail by cutting on top and bottom (and on both sides, of course) to your reference lines. The top and bottom centerlines should mark the widest area of the tail from top to bottom. Next, before you finish the shape of the tail, smooth the base of the tail into the back of the body (the borderline may now be cut away). Then, gently round out the sides of the tail, carving away the guidelines except for top and side centerlines. Finally you may taper the tail to your satisfaction by cutting down the top and bottom centerlines

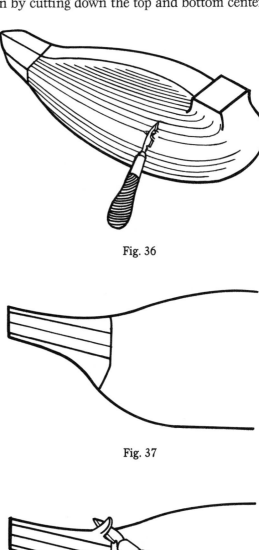

Fig. 36

Fig. 37

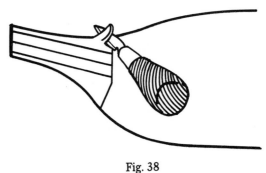

Fig. 38

15

so the tail flattens toward the tip. Don't carve mechanically, but keep in mind always the final shape you want to achieve.

When the tail is finished, you are ready to attach the head. First, roughly sand the head using a piece of medium sandpaper. The sanding at this point may be finished more or less to your satisfaction. Just be careful not to overdo it. Don't sand out of the carving the shape that you worked so hard to carve in! This is easier to do than you think, if you don't pay attention while you are sanding.

Also lightly sand the two surfaces that you are going to glue, this time using a flat sanding block (a small, flat block of wood will do). Sand the surfaces flat; this way, when they are glued together the seam will hardly show and the bond will be stronger.

For gluing I recommend a quick-setting epoxy glue, found in most good hardware stores. This sets up in ten to fifteen minutes. Gluing the head to the body is quite simple. Begin by mixing the glue on the neck seat of the body, spreading it out sufficiently. Then place the head on the neck seat. Firmly press down while twisting the head back and forth to even out the glue. Next, align the base of the neck very carefully with the outlines of the neck seat, keeping your pressure on the head firm. When the head is placed exactly where you want it, let go of it and allow the glue to dry. The heads of working decoys are often doweled into the bodies for strength, but if your decoy is meant for decorative purposes (most decoys these days spend their lives on coffee tables or mantels of fireplaces), this method of gluing should be more than sufficient to hold on the head.

Now all the carving that is left involves smoothing the neck into the neck seat. First draw four guidelines across the joint between neck and neck seat. These guidelines should be at right angles to the neck-seat joint and should be centered between the four corners. See Fig. 39. Now start carving on one of the corners and carve to the guidelines you just drew, on either side. Do this at all four corners, taking care to make the neck smoothly rounded and looking the same on both sides of the decoy. Take your time. You are almost through. Don't let your excitement overcome your common sense, or you may ruin all your previous work.

Now check the entire decoy. When you are satisfied that it is smoothly rounded throughout, symmetrical (the same on both sides) and exactly the way you want it, give the entire decoy a fine sanding. Except for the painting and the setting in of the eyes, you have just created a Mallard decoy. Congratulations on a job well done!

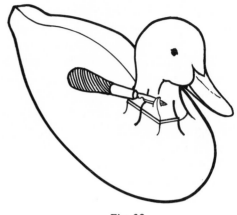

Fig. 39

Setting the Eyes

Glass eyes for duck decoys are widely available from many woodcraft suppliers (including the present author). Setting them into the head of your decoy is really pretty simple. Gather some fine sawdust and get some common yellow wood glue and a mixing can. You can make an excellent wood paste by mixing about 40% glue with about 60% fine sawdust and adding just a little water to keep the paste from sticking while you're mixing it. This paste is not only good for setting the eyes of a decoy but it also comes in handy as a general wood filler.

When you have mixed your paste, fill the eye holes with it. Then simply push the eyes into the paste-filled holes. The paste should ooze out around the eyes if it was packed into the holes properly. Take care that the eyes are pushed in to the proper depth and are set at the right angle. Next wet one of your fingers and gently wipe the paste around the eyes, sealing the space between the eye hole and the eye. Wipe away any excess paste. Don't worry about getting any wood paste on the eyes. It can easily be wiped off without hurting them. Even if the paste dries on an eye, it's no problem to get it off later.

Once the eyes are in place, double check to see that they are set deep enough. Do this by looking down at the top of the head. The eyes shouldn't look as though they are bulging, and they should be directly opposite each other and facing in the right direction. This direction may be varied; just be sure that they look natural. The eyes are the main focal point of a decoy. They add life and expression and make your carving more realistic. Learn to set the eyes to get a striking effect, and you will have learned another secret of woodcarving.

Painting Your Decoy

Now that you have carved a Mallard decoy, you will want to paint it to look like a Mallard. Painting a woodcarving in realistic detail, like all fine art, takes a long time to learn. Since decoys, however, were originally used for the practical purpose of hunting, they were not generally painted in any great detail. It is not difficult to paint a decoy in this fashion. The following tips should get you started.

First, be sure that you have all the materials you will need. Most important of all is good reference material. Color photographs, drawings, anything that accurately shows the bird you are portraying, is essential. If you have a chance to observe live birds, so much the better! I wouldn't even consider painting a decoy unless I had gathered good reference material.

Also necessary are, of course, paints and brushes. I recommend acrylic paints because they are easy to work with. For a Mallard, you will need the following colors: Titanium white, Mars black, raw umber, yellow oxide, emerald green, burnt sienna and burnt umber. I also recommend using two brushes, #6 and #10 round red sable brushes.

Before you apply the final coat of paint, it is a good idea to seal the surface of the wood with a primer. You can make the primer yourself by simply mixing some of your black and white paints to make a medium gray. Paint the entire decoy with a few coats of this primer, allowing the paint to dry between coats. When the final coat is thoroughly dry, gently sand the entire surface smooth with #220 sandpaper. Be very careful not to scratch the glass eyes with the sandpaper. On the other hand, don't worry about getting paint on the eyes. In fact, I always paint right over the eyes. Later the paint can be cleaned off by brushing a little water on the eyes and where necessary scraping gently with your knife. When the decoy has been sanded, gently buff it with a paper towel, and the sealed surface is ready for painting.

Fig. 40 shows how your paint colors are distributed on the decoy. Supplement this guide with your reference material.

Here are a few more tips. Begin painting at the rear of your decoy and work your way forward. This way it may be easier to shape the borders where the different colors meet, and you can use the head of the decoy as a handle to hold the carving in place as you paint the largest portion of the bird. Also be aware that Fig. 40 is a very rough guide. Not all the colors indicated there should be mixed the same way for different areas, and different modes of applying the paint help in different areas. The back of a Mallard is usually a shade or two darker than the sides, although both are shades of gray. Also, the raw umber areas should be applied in several light coats. Don't try to fill in all the color with the first coat.

Painting more realistically will take practice. Above all, study your reference material. If you don't know what a real male Mallard looks like, you won't be able to paint your decoy to resemble one. Closer study will reveal interesting details not usually observed by most people. For instance, the ring on a Mallard's neck doesn't really extend all the way to the back.

Like carving a decoy, painting one takes care and practice. Go over the guidelines I've given, be patient and use a little common sense, and you should do a fine job.

Painting Guide: Mallard Decoy

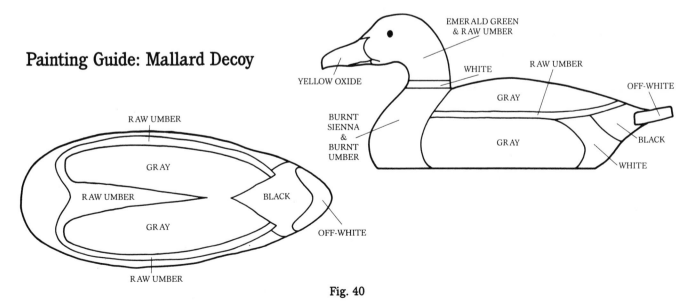

Fig. 40